KOBE BRYANT

RICHARD J. BRENNER

Beech Tree
New York

AN EAST END PUBLISHING BOOK

Kobe Bryant had a wonderful
childhood, growing up in a secure
and loving family, with his two sisters,
Shaya and Sharia, his mother, Pam,
and his father, Joe "Jelly Bean" Bryant.
"He's always been there for me," says
Kobe, speaking of his father, who
played professional basketball for 16
seasons. "We can talk about anything.
I love him to death."

By the time Kobe was six, his father's eight-year career in the National Basketball Association had come to an end, so the Bryants packed their bags and moved to Italy, where Joe started playing in a European basketball league. "It was difficult at first because I couldn't speak Italian," says Kobe. "But my sisters and I got together after school to teach each other new words we had learned. Within a few months, I was able to speak Italian pretty well."

Kobe also learned to play basketball, partly by watching his father, but mostly by studying tapes of NBA games and then going out and practicing what he had just seen. "I was like a computer," says Kobe, who spent countless hours practicing his favorite moves. "I would watch everybody, from Oscar Robertson to Michael Jordan. I'd copy their pet moves and add them to my game. I retrieved information that would benefit my game."

During the Bryants' eight-year stay in Europe, Kobe also learned the basic skills of basketball from Italian coaches. "In Italy, they teach you the ABCs of basketball," says Kobe, who returned to America in time to start high school. "When I came back to the States and saw everybody dunking and doing fancy things, I just figured I'd pick up those skills. If you have the fundamentals down at an early age, you can advance much quicker."

Kobe advanced so quickly during his four years at Lower Merion High School, that he became one of the top prep school players in the country. "Kobe Bryant is the most complete player in the class of 1996," said one highly respected scout. "What he can't do, can't be done."

In his senior season, Kobe averaged 31 points, 12 rebounds, 6.5 assists, 4 blocks and 4 steals per game, while leading the Lower Merion Aces to the Pennsylvania Class AAAA state championship. And for the first time in his life, Kobe was finally able to out-play his dad in their one-on-one games.

"I had to make up certain rules," says Joe Bryant, laughing. "We only played a low-post game, and I refereed and kept score. When Kobe hit five baskets in a row and asked the score, I'd tell him, 'I'm up one. Dad's up one.' I'm always up one."

Kobe not only had super skills on the basketball court, he was also a superior student and had a basketful of college scholarships from which to choose. Kobe, though, decided to bypass college and play in the NBA. "I just went with what I felt in my heart," says Kobe. "Playing in the NBA has been my goal since I was in ninth grade."

Kobe, who plays nonstop, just like his favorite cartoon character, the Road Runner, wound up playing for the Los Angeles Lakers. "He has a wonderful way about him," said Lakers' executive Jerry West, who is a former NBA superstar. "This is a uniquely nice kid and a uniquely talented kid."

Kobe, who became only the sixth
player to make the big leap from
high school to the NBA, didn't get a
whole lot of playing time during his
first season with the Lakers. But he
did sparkle like a Roman Candle
during All-Star Weekend, scoring a
Rookie Game–record 31 points in the

Schick Rookie Game before going on to win the 1997 Nestlé Crunch Slam Dunk Championship. Kobe soared so high and dunked so spectacularly that even the other contestants stood and cheered as he lifted the winning trophy over his head.

Kobe spent the following offseason taking college courses at UCLA and working out every day so that he would be ready to have a much bigger impact in his second season with the Lakers. The results were immediate and stunning and his high-flying style of play was so sensational and his personality so positive that fans around the league voted him a starter for the Western Conference All-Star Team.

The prospect of playing in his first NBA All-Star Game and matching up against Michael Jordan made Kobe feel like a little boy opening a great big birthday present. "It's a thrill to be playing with all the greatest players in the league," said Kobe, who was the youngest player ever picked to play in an NBA All-Star Game. "Playing against Michael Jordan is the ultimate challenge. It's going to be fun. I can't wait."

Kobe rewarded his fans by scoring a team-high 18 points, including one super-spectacular, 360-degree slam that earned him a standing ovation from the capacity crowd at New York's Madison Square Garden. Kobe finished his second season as the highest-scoring reserve in the league, but is looking for much bigger results in the future. "What I'm doing is chasing perfection, and if I don't get it, I'm going to get *this* close."

Kobe also knows that being an NBA star makes him a role model for millions of kids, and he's totally fine with that responsibility. "It's fun. You get to meet some children in a positive way. It's cool. I love it. I love having kids come up to me. They can relate to me because I'm a kid myself right now."

More exciting, photo-filled books from America's favorite sportswriter

NOW AVAILABLE
BASKETBALL SUPERSTARS ALBUM 1999
By Richard J. Brenner

Includes 16 pages of full-color photos of the top players in the NBA, plus full-page biographies and complete career stats. Also includes predictions for the 1998-1999 season and a chance to challenge the expert with your own predictions.

FOOTBALL SUPERSTARS ALBUM 1998
By Richard J. Brenner

Includes 16 pages of full-color shots of the top players in the NFL, plus full-page biographies and complete career stats. Also includes predictions for the 1998 season and a chance to challenge the expert with your own predictions.

MICHAEL JORDAN
By Richard J. Brenner

A photo-biography of the greatest player in the history of basketball.
Filled with lots of exciting photos and featuring an easy-to-read format.

COMING SOON
BASEBALL SUPERSTARS ALBUM 1999
By Richard J. Brenner

Includes 16 pages of full-color shots of the top players in the major leagues, plus full-page biographies and complete career stats. Also includes predictions for the 1999 season and a chance to challenge the expert with your own predictions.

Photo Credits: The cover photo as well as the photos on pages 1 and 18 were taken by Jed Jacobsohn/AllSport. The photos on pages 2, 6, 12, and 26 were taken by Michael Zito/SportsChrome. The photo on page 4 was taken by Rocky Widner. The photo on page 9 was taken by David Taylor/AllSport. The photo on page 15 was taken by John Gichigi/AllSport. The center spread on pages 16 and 17 was taken by Brian Spurlock. The photo on page 21 was taken by Vincent Laforet/AllSport. The photos on pages 24 and 32 were taken by Andrew D. Bernstein/NBA AllSport. The photo on page 31 was taken by David Taylor/AllSport.

Cover layout by Jim Wasserman.

Published by Beech Tree Books, a division of William Morrow and Company, Inc.
1350 Avenue of the Americas, New York, NY 10019
www.williammorrow.com

Printed in the United States of America

First Beech Tree Edition, 1999
ISBN 0-688-16585-0

10 9 8 7 6 5 4 3 2 1